To Manuela,
who taught
me that wishes
come true.

Dedicado también
a mi querido padre
Ernesto Cavour.

Manu and the Mystery of the lowercase b

By: Inti F. Cavour
Pictures by: Raquel Rivera Safadi

Once upon a time, there was a little girl who was learning how to read and write.

Her name was Manu. One day, while Manu was doing her homework, she noticed that the letters b and d were all mixed up.

She could not tell them apart! Which one was b? Which one was d? What a muddle!

This is a real mystery that needs to be solved!" Manu said, "The mystery of the lowercase b!"

She decided to solve this mystery herself, and her good friends, the letters of the Alphabet, agreed to help her.

So, she stood up and jumped into her homework to meet them.

Once Manu was with her friends, Letter A called the other letters of the Alphabet and asked them to get in line.

It was then that they realized that lowercase Letters b and d were missing!

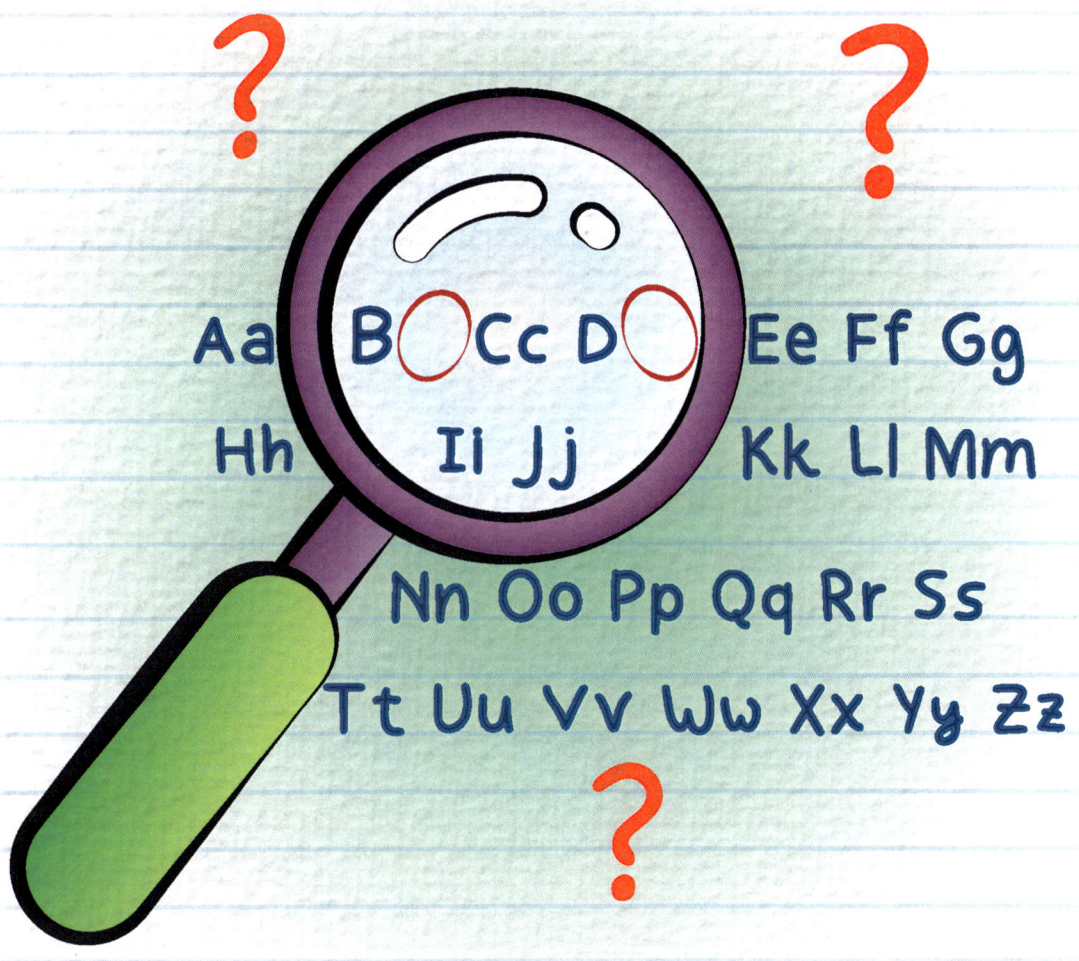

Manu saw some footprints on the floor, so she decided to follow them.

The footprints took her to where Letters b and d were playing with blocks.

When the Letters b and d saw Manu, they grabbed her hands and started to dance with her.

When they stopped dancing and spinning around, Manu could see that b and d were all mixed up again!

" So, which one of you is Letter b?" Manu asked.

"It is up to you to find out," one of them answered. But was it Letter b or d? Manu couldn't tell.

So, she put both her thumbs up and remembered that the left hand formed a lowercase b while the right hand formed a lowercase d.

There was just one small problem...

Manu couldn't tell which hand was right and which one was left! "This is harder than I thought," she sighed.

Letters b and d felt very sad too, and so they gave Manu a big hug and asked her to try again.

"Don't worry, take your time," they said.

"I have an idea!" Manu shouted "Let's do the diaper trick! One of you wears a diaper, and the other one has a belly! Right?"

"Oh no," Manu cried again "Which of you has a belly? Where does the diaper go?"

Poor Manu, the truth was that none of the letters wanted to wear diapers, so Letters b and d did everything to confuse her.

"These Letters of the Alphabet are very tricky," Manu groaned, worried about making another mistake.

"You can do this!" said one of the letters.

"Don't give up now!" said the other letter, encouraging Manu.

"That is true! I can do it! I never give up and I won't start today," Manu replied with a big smile. So, she took a ruler and a pencil and started measuring the letters.

"I've got it! You are the lowercase b," Manu shouted with glee.

"Yes! You're right! I'm the lowercase b! But tell me, how did you figure it out?" Letter b asked.

"My dear b, when I took a closer look at you, I saw that you look a lot like your big brother, uppercase B." Then Manu called uppercase B.

"I just put a half-circle on top of you and there we go! You look just like your big brother!"

"That is true! Hooray!" everyone cheered. Now the mystery of the lowercase b is solved, thanks to a little girl who did not let confusion or fear of making mistakes stop her from completing her important mission!

The end.

Written by: Inti F. Cavour
Illustrated by: Raquel Rivera Safadi
Copyright © 2022 Inti F. Cavour
All rights reserved. No portion of this book may be reproduced in any form without permission from the publisher, except as permitted by U.S. copyright law. For permissions contact: icavour10@gmail.com

Made in United States
North Haven, CT
05 March 2025

66484587R00015